Boats of Life

SUE DENNEY

ILLUSTRATIONS BY JINGO DE LA ROSA

CrossBooks™
A Division of LifeWay
1663 Liberty Drive
Bloomington, IN 47403
www.crossbooks.com
Phone: 1-866-879-0502

First published by CrossBooks 4/19/2012

ISBN: 978-1-4627-1549-7 (sc)

Printed in the United States of America

This book is printed on acid-free paper.

Any people depicted in stock imagery provided by Thinkstock are models, and such images are being used for illustrative purposes only.

Certain stock imagery © Thinkstock.

Because of the dynamic nature of the Internet, any web addresses or links contained in this book may have changed since publication and may no longer be valid. The views expressed in this work are solely those of the author and do not necessarily reflect the views of the publisher, and the publisher hereby disclaims any responsibility for them.

CROSSBOOKS
PUBLISHING

Contents

The Church's Boat

Our churches are made up of people traveling on boats of life. People who are suffering the pain of depression, unhappy marriages, unhappy lives due to childhood abuse, rape, and domestic violence. They are suffering within themselves because of shame, and fear that someone will find out they are not the happy Christian they think they are suppose to be as a Child of God.

When was the last time you heard a sermon giving people hope who are victims of abuse. Offering them a ticket onto God's Boat that will carry them to peace and happiness through the storms of life.

The Bible tells about some of God's people going through storms. Each time God showed up to rescue them. God is our rescuer from the pains of abuse. He provides us boats found in His Word to find healing and peace.

Noah's Boat

GENESIS 6–9:11

"The Lord saw how great man's wickedness on the earth had become and that every inclination of the thoughts of the heart was on evil all the time. The Lord was grieved that he had made man on earth and his heart was filled with pain." Genesis 6:5-6

God decided to wipe all mankind from the face of the earth except Noah, who was a righteous man. God told Noah to build a big boat. He worked on this boat for many years building it just like God told him to. People laughed at him and thought he was crazy for building a boat. The day it started raining, the people realized Noah was not so crazy, but it was too late. God rescued Noah and his family and two of every kind of animal living on the earth at that time.

When you are drowning in flood waters from the pains of sexual abuse, physical abuse, rape, and domestic violence, it is hard to see the boat. When your abuser attends church each Sunday, it is hard to see the boat. When your abuser is a well-respected member of the church, it is hard to see the boat.

Some children in our church's Sunday School classes are victims of abuse. They need a boat to protect them from the rain of an abuser.

Some teen-agers in the youth group are victims of abuse. They are looking for their rescue boat through drugs, alcohol, sex and crime.

Adults in small groups are drowning in past memories. Women are drowning in the pain of being raped or victims of domestic violence.

God has a boat to rescue His children who are drowning in pain and unhappiness. God chose Noah as the boat builder because he was a righteous man. God has chosen boat builders in His church who have to be willing to build the boat to rescue people drowning in the pain of abuse.

Jonah's Boat

Many times Christians who are victims of abuse, rape or domestic violence get on the boat of life to run from the pain. The pain becomes very intense just as the storm became intense during Jonah's boat ride. The waves of memories crash onto the boat over and over again.

You hide in the bottom of the boat and sleep just like Jonah, hoping the pain will go away. When you wake up, the storm continues to threaten your life. The pain never leaves, until finally, you are thrown overboard into the stormy sea, waiting for death.

Instead of death, God sends a rescue, a big fish. Jonah stayed in the belly of the big fish for three days. While Jonah was in the belly of the fish, he prayed to God and found peace.

Christian victims of abuse need to find peace in the belly of the big fish. Peace comes when you relive the memory and feel the pains associated with the abuse. This can be a scary and difficult time while being in the belly of past memories.

Just as God rescued Jonah out the belly of the big fish, God will rescue His child and bring healing and peace to their lives. Once Christians have found healing and peace, they can change the direction of life and begin their journey to the "City of Nineveh", just like Jonah.

God cares for His children just like he cared for the City of Nineveh. He wants His children to be free of pain and unhappiness. He will bring peace and healing during the storm if we are willing to follow His plan.

Jesus' Boat

Matthew 8:23-27

Victims of childhood abuse, rape and domestic violence fill our churches. They are pastors, staff leaders, deacons, teachers, choir members, as well as countless others. As they sit in the boat of life, just like the Disciples, everything seems alright, until the storm hits. Storms of depression, anger, sadness, and fear violently rock their boat. The fear of being destroyed by the waves that grows stronger and stronger.

Christian victims can go to Jesus and say, "Lord save me, I going to die". All they see are the waves hitting the boat of life threatening to destroy them.

Jesus says to the Christian victim, "Why are you fearful, you of little faith". He looks at the pain of childhood abuse, rape, and domestic violence and rebukes the storm and brings peace and calm to their lives.

Paul's Boat

ACTS 27:1-44

Paul became a prisoner for preaching the truth about Jesus. His enemies accused him of telling lies and wanted to see him dead. His trial would be far away, across the sea. While he was on the journey, his boat was destroyed by the storm, but he was not hurt.

Victims of childhood abuse, rape and domestic violence become prisoners of lies. Lies planted by the enemy that wants to see them dead.

During the journey of life, storms come and destroy the boats of life. The storms of depression, sadness, anger and fear threaten to shipwreck their boats. Paul was shipwrecked on an island where the local people showed him extraordinary kindness. They took care of all his needs.

God sends people to show His shipwrecked children extraordinary kindness. Christian counselors to help them relive the memories of abuse and rape. Helping them through the pain to find peace and happiness. Ministers and teachers to guide them to a new boat where God takes care of their needs.

Paul ministered to the ship's crew and people on the island. He continued to preach the truth about Jesus until his death.

Life with pain and unhappiness is like a shipwrecked on the shores of defeat. But when you climb on board God's boat, He will guide you through the storms so you can tell others the truth how Jesus rescue you from the storms of abuse.

God's Boat

God wants you to have a healthy and happy life. You can have a personal relationship with Him by:

Admitting to God that you are a sinner

Repent and turn away from your sins

Believe by faith that Jesus is God's Son and accept Jesus gift of forgiveness from sin

Confess your faith in Jesus Christ as Savior and Lord

If you are choosing to believe that Jesus died for your sins and to receive new life through Him, pray a prayer asking Jesus to forgive you of yours sins and to live in your heart.

CPSIA information can be obtained
at www.ICGtesting.com
Printed in the USA
LVIC040352080512

280773LV00001B

9781462715497